TRENDLINE TRADING

How to Master Trendlines Trading Using Candlestick Chart Patterns Analysis to identify Potential Entries and Exits in the Financial Markets

George Milton

Disclaimer Notice:

The information contained in this book does not constitute advice and should not be construed, directly or indirectly, as an offer, request or inducement to buy or sell any type of currency, financial products or instruments, nor as a recommendation to invest or to participate in an investment or trading strategy.

The content is for information purpose only, and does not take into account situations, goals or specific financial needs of the readers, so it should not be used to make specific investments decisions.

By reading this book, you accept that the author does not guarantee, endorse or take responsibility for the reliability, accuracy or completeness of the information, nor will he be liable for any type of direct or indirect loss, derived from any decision made based on the information provided.

It should be noted that trading can be very speculative and therefore generate profits and also losses, and it is advisable to have adequate knowledge before risking your capital on a trade. Should you need further guidance, do well to seek the services of a professional trader.

TABLE OF CONTENTS

CHAPTER 1

TECHNICAL ANALYSIS BASICS

To be successful in market trading, you must learn to analyze and generate forecasts for price movements. The market price is influenced by a wide range of various factors, all of which we literally cannot know. A question arises: in this case, how is forecast made possible? Technical analysis, one of the most fundamental and essential types of market analysis, provides an answer to this question.

What is Technical Analysis?

Technical analysis is a method of forecasting price changes by analyzing price charts of the time frame. A technical analysis is about the analysis of price charts. To continue the story about the basics of technical analysis, you must first familiarize yourself with the main chart types.

Main Chart Types

All changes in the price are reflected on the charts, which are of several types:

Tick Chart

Tick chart reflects each market price change on the chart and is not time bound. As long as there are many trades in the market, there are many price changes in a minute. The chart is too chaotic to analyze, often used by scalpers for day trading.

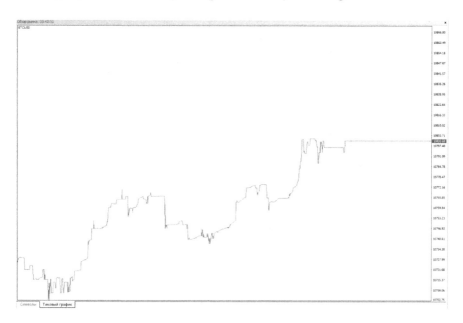

Line Chart

Line chart is the simplest chart, most often drawn on the closing prices of each time period. It looks like a solid angular line. It practically reflects the outcome of the competition between bulls and bears in each time period and also shows the general direction of price movements.

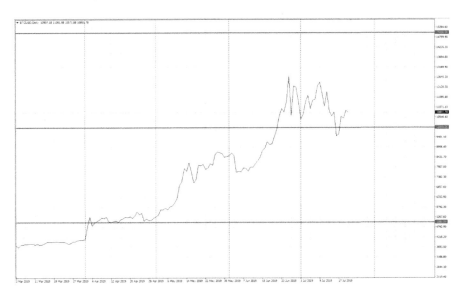

Bar Chart

Bar chart reflects price changes in a compact way, each period is seen as a bar showing the opening and closing price, high and low. This information is enough to work with such a chart.

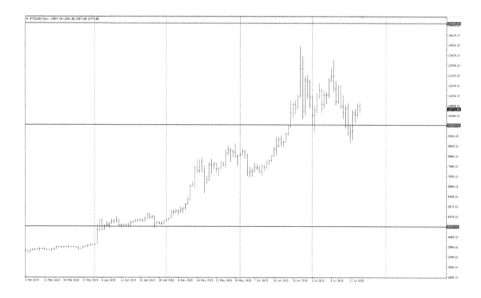

Candle Chart

The candlestick chart is also called a Japanese candlestick chart. It is drawn similar to the bar chart, but the end result is called the body of the candle. This chart is more demonstrative since the bodies are colored.

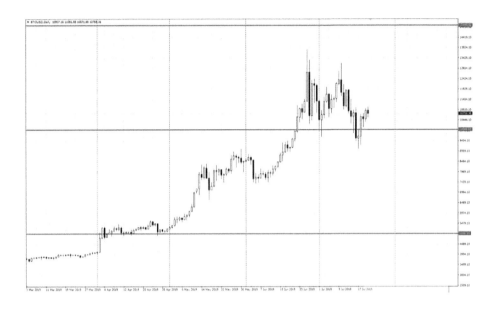

Postulates of Technical Analysis

The Price Reflects Everything

The idea is that the market takes into account any factor that could influence the price and immediately includes it in the price, which is reflected on the chart. In other words, the price chart at any moment reflects and reacts to all the factors that influence it: economic and political rumours, expectations, etc.

Price Movements Are Subject to Trends

This means that in the market, there are periods of time in which the price moves predominantly in one direction (up or down). In other words, a trend is a one-way price movement. The reasons for the appearance of a trend can be economic, political and other factors. The existing trend is believed to be more likely to continue than to change and will remain in place until it weakens and shows explicit signs of the next change.

Depending on the length, trends can be divided into 3 types:

- Short-term trends exist from a few days to several weeks.
- Medium-term trends exist from one to several months.
- Long-term trends last from 6 months.

History Repeats Itself

There are certain laws in the market. This means that the rules that used to work in the past will probably work in the future and today. The analysis of historical data allows to carry out not only technical analysis, but also statistical ones. Based on the statistics collected and analyzed from the above time frame, the behavior of the market can be forecast with some certainty. And although the market can change and has its peculiarities at certain times, in general the laws work.

Trend and Its Types in Technical Analysis

As a famous market saying goes, the trend is your friend. In technical analysis, we highlight 3 types of trends: an uptrend, a downtrend, and a flat.

Uptrend

An uptrend means that the price is moving up. The main condition for the existence of the uptrend is that each next high is higher than the previous one, as well as each next low is also higher than the previous one. The trend keeps going up until the trade complies with this rule, but as soon as the next high or low is below the previous one, the trend ends. Through the local minima, we draw a horizontal line that we call support.

In an uptrend, the support line is called the trend line and it is down. Through the local maxima we draw another line called resistance. When support and resistance lines are parallel, a so-called price channel is formed.

A price channel is the price fluctuation between parallel support and resistance lines within the existing trend. The main rule of uptrend trading is to buy at the support level and exit your positions at the resistance level.

Downward Trend

A downtrend is a downward trend in prices. The main condition for a downtrend to exist is that each next high is lower than the previous one, and the same with the lows. The downtrend continues until some high or low is higher than the previous one, then we consider the trend to be over. Through the local highs, we draw the resistance line.

In the downtrend, it is called a trend line and it is high. Through the local minima, we draw a straight line called the support line. A price channel is formed when the resistance and support lines are parallel (descending, in this case). The main rule of trading in a downtrend is to sell at resistance and close your positions at support.

Range

A range or bottom, is a price fluctuation in a sideways range when there is no significant growth or clear decline. Price changes on a floor are restricted by the support line from below and the resistance line from above, the lines form a price channel. When the price breaks out of the channel up or down, the floor ends.

From the edges of a flat, you can trade up and down equally. The main rule is to sell at the resistance line and close your positions at the support line, and vice versa (buy at the support line and close your positions at the resistance line).

Support and Resistance Levels

Important technical analysis instruments are the support and resistance lines, that is, the lines drawn between the important maximums or minimums and that have a specific price value.

- Support is a price area where active buying can pause the trend or reverse it to decline.
- Resistance is a price area where active selling can pause the trend or reverse it to rise.

Support and resistance lines are drawn through those points on the chart from where the correction starts. The longer the term, the more important the levels drawn will be.

The principle of level polarity: if the resistance level is broken and the price rises, the level becomes the support. And vice versa, if the price falls below the support line, the latter becomes the resistance level.

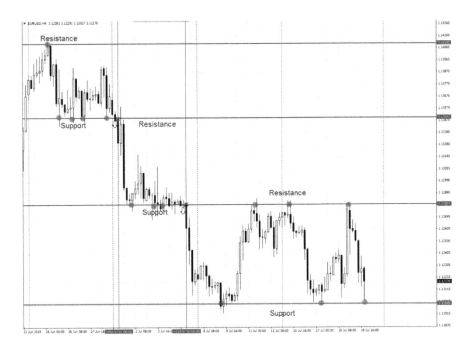

Technical Analysis Chart Patterns

As a result of long-term studies of the market, it was observed that periodically price patterns appear on the chart that allow forecasting future price behavior. There are patterns that indicate a reversal of the trend and patterns that indicate its continuation. It is worth noting here that there is no 100% guarantee that the forecast will come to fruition. However, it is high enough to use patterns in trading.

The most famous price patterns are:

Head and Shoulders, Inverted Head and Shoulders Chart Patterns

Head and Shoulders, Inverted Head and Shoulders are reversal patterns that form at high and low prices.

Double Top, Double Bottom Chart Patterns

Double Top, Double Bottom are reversal patterns that form at high and low prices.

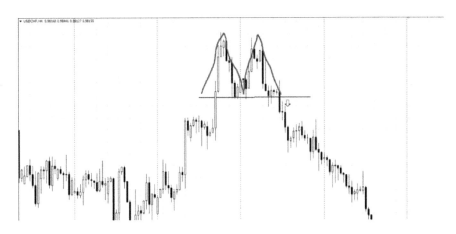

Triple Top, Triple Bottom Chart Patterns

Triple Top, Triple Bottom are reversal patterns that form at the price highs and lows.

Wedge Chart Pattern

Wedge is a reversal pattern that forms at high and low prices.

Diamond Chart Pattern

Diamond is a reversal pattern that forms at high and low prices.

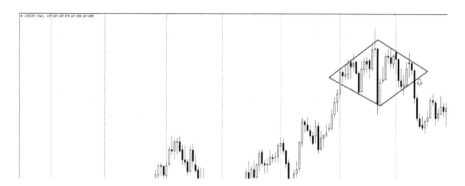

Flag Chart Pattern

Flag chart pattern is a trend continuation pattern.

Triangle Chart Pattern

Triangle is a trend continuation pattern.

Technical Analysis Using Indicators

Ever since computers were first used for trading, a wide range of various indicators have been created that help traders perform complex market analysis.

Technical indicators are mathematical functions based on price or volumes. They may not only help analyze the market, but also directly give trading signals. Some indicators work well in a trend, some work well in a range. There are also universal indicators.

Moving Average (MA)

Moving Average (MA) is an indicator of the average price movement. It is a computer analysis instrument that smooths out price fluctuations by averaging over a certain period of time.

Moving Average Convergence-Divergence (MACD)

Moving Average Convergence Divergence (MACD) is a combination of three exponentially smoothed moving averages. The indicator looks like a histogram with a signal line on it.

Bollinger Bands (BB)

Bollinger Bands (BB) help define the moment of the market's transition from calm to active state and vice versa. The indicator is placed on the price and is made up of three moving averages with fixed deviations.

The Relative Strength Index (RSI)

The Relative Strength Index (RSI) is an oscillator that measures the relative strength of the market, comparing absolute values of market growth and decline.

Stochastic Oscillator

Stochastic Oscillator uses the following condition: in an uptrend, the closing price points to the highs of the time frame, and in a downtrend, to the lows.

Ichimoku Kinko Hyo (Ichimoku)

Ichimoku Kinko Hyo is a complex indicator made up of 5 lines, 3 of which are moving averages and 2 are their derivatives. Ichimoku not only defines the presence of a trend, but also provides information on the location of support and resistance areas.

Fibonacci Levels

Fibonacci represents the approximate correction levels on the chart, calculating them on the basis of the row of numbers, discovered by the famous mathematician.

Technical analysis is the bare minimum that serious trading provides. In the same way, we need the alphabet to learn to read and the multiplication table to learn to count. And although knowledge of technical analysis in itself does not guarantee success in trading, it serves as a starting point for mastering all the secrets of the market and forming your own trading system.

CHAPTER 2

DRAWDOWN AND MARKET MOVEMENTS

Anyone involved in trading should be familiar with terms such as Margin Call and Stop Out Level. Each person has come to know it in his own way. Some practically got acquainted with them, strongly closed their losing positions, while some in theory, studied the basics of trading.

If you haven't heard these terms yet, a short lecture perhaps, will make you think hard about the consequences of irrational and overly emotional trading.

Margin call is a notification from your broker, requiring you to additionally replenish your security deposit.

If after a Margin call the trader does not deposit his heir account, and the losses continue to grow, then after the price reaches a certain level, the Stop Out procedure will be started. This means that the broker will close some or all open positions on the account. Margin Call and Stop Out, on the other hand, are not as disastrous as the trader's actions that lead to them.

One of those actions could be related to thoughtless trading operations based on no strategy or tactics, no risk and no money management. An example of such actions can be the trading of all capital both in periods of high volatility and in a calm market. At such times, the trader is more of a gambler, hoping for a quick win.

However, in most cases, a loss of the deposit is caused by prolonged drawdown and irrational attempts to escape from it. Primary drawdowns, in turn, are caused by deviations from the trading strategy (if any) and increases in trading volumes.

What is a Drawdown?

A drawdown is a decrease in the balance and equity of the trading account. To put it more simply, a reduction. Reductions or drawdowns can be of two types: floating and fixed.

Floating and Fixed Drawdown

The Drawdown is an aggregate loss of all open positions. We highlight here that the trades we are discussing are still open. For example, the trader opened a position, and then the market situation started to develop against the forecasts, so the trade made a loss. This loss will constitute the floating reduction.

Also, such a reduction is called floating or temporary because a day or two later, the situation can change for better or worse. However, as soon as the trade is closed, the drawdown changes from a floating to a fixed one.

A fixed drawdown in turn can be of the following types:

- Absolute drawdown.
- Maximum.
- Relative.

Absolute Drawdown

Absolute Drawdown is the largest loss compared to the initial sum in the trading account. To calculate the absolute drawdown, we must deduct the minimum value reached by the yield curve from the initial sum on the deposit.

Example 1

The initial sum is $10,000. During the trading time, the sum has never been less than $7,000. So we deduct $7,000 from $10,000, getting $3,000.

This value will be considered the current absolute drawdown. Why do we call it current? The thing is that the sum in the account could decrease below $7,000, and the absolute drawdown will change. In general, this value is not very informative neither for the trader nor for the investor who analyzes the manager's statistics.

Maximum Drawdown

Maximum Drawdown is an indicator calculated as the difference between the current maximum and the minimum of the deposit. It should be noted that for the calculation, we do not take the minimum value of the deposit in its history, but the minimum value that the deposit reached when reaching the maximum.

Example 2

The initial deposit was $10,000. It then fell to $8,000 after a series of unlucky trades; it then grew to $15,000 and then decreased to $13,000.

In this case, the maximum deposit sum was $15,000 and the minimum value after the maximum was $13,000. So the maximum drawdown will be the difference between $15,000 and $13,000, or $2,000.

Relative Drawdown

The drawdown is calculated as the above index, but in percentage, not in currency.

Reasons for Drawdowns

I will keep repeating that bad trading can be explained by wrong choice of strategy and lack of systematic risk and money management. However, even if the trader has all of these trading elements, he can be betrayed by his personal psychology or his discipline.

Errors will be revealed by increases in trading volume, unreasonable and chaotic buying and selling, closing and using the Martingale. Of course, all of this could work, but it will not be systematic.

If you have withdrawals too often, you should be thinking something like, *Am I trading the right way*? I mean, you can plan your profits and losses if your trading system is in harmony with the market and your money management helps you escape drawdowns quickly and rack up profits.

If your trading account is affected, first and foremost, you need to accept it. Any trader has a drawdown at some point, and his presence on the account is practically normal, the question is in its size.

An experienced trader will never let a drawdown go too deep. On the contrary, a beginner can easily lose 40% or even 70% of the deposit, sticking to lost trades and adding new ones. If he doesn't agree with the axiom that a drawdown is normal and starts proving the market wrong, he can simply make the problem worse and lose all his capital in the end.

For a beginner trader, I would recommend deciding what sum of a draw is normal for them and what is not. This decision will undoubtedly be subjective. For some people, a loss will be normal if it does not exceed 10%, while others can easily cope with a 50% loss.

I would highlight the following levels:

- Up to 15%: a normal drawdown.
- 16% - 30% - do not panic yet, but the time has come to reduce the risks and intensity of trading. The situation and dynamics of the market, as well as the status of your trading instrument, should be reviewed.

- 31% - 60% - the end is near. If the drawdown is greater than 30%, you should stop trading and pause, then come back with your revised strategy.

I must remind you that these numbers are here for clarity only. They can change according to the trader's temperament and trading style. However, in my opinion, a loss of 50% of the deposit and more is unacceptable.

When the comfortable level of drawdown is decided, it's time to analyze your trade. In this, an account statement or your trader's journal (if you keep track of all trades) can be of great help. After analyzing the trade, we will find out if the series of losing trades was consistent with your strategy or not, if it was systematic or not, if you have exceeded your risk and volume limits.

Based on my own experience and that of other people, I could say that 8 out of 10 losing trades can be explained by a lack (or violation) of a trading strategy or money management methods, as well as exceeding risk limits.

How to Escape from a Drawdown?

So now we are getting closer to the part that is why you have started reading this. Once again, withdrawal from an account is a natural situation that you will hardly avoid. However, you can always optimize and minimize your influence on the account. All this is quite easy to do. You have to follow the money and risk management rules and your strategy. To most people, my words will seem trivial. This is because not all traders have a strict financial plan, trading strategy, money and risk management systems. Therefore, the first step out of the drawdown will be to add the aforementioned to your negotiation. However, what do we do if the account had a drawdown and a very serious one?

There is a law: the deeper the drawdown, the longer it will take you to get out of it. If the trader was not lucky enough to lose 50% of the deposit in 2-3 trades, it is unlikely that he will restore the capital in an equally short time.

On the Internet, you can find a lot of information about Martingale averaging, blocking, and usage. However, the defenders of these methods are also there. Not wanting to start an argument, I will say that both averaging and blocking can be very useful to the trader if they know the tricks.

The Main Nuances of Escaping from a Drawdown

Imagine that the trader opened a trade to buy, but the price started to decline, so the trade turned losing. To compensate for the loss, the trader opens another trade with the Duplicate Volume parcel. But unfortunately the second trade is also losing. In such a situation, many beginners begin to panic, turning to experienced traders for help, wasting time and increasing drawdown.

Here, the trader needs to open some blocking trades to limit the growth of losses. A lockout will give them some time to analyze, calm down, and develop tactics to make up for losses. However, a padlock is neither a panacea nor a Grail. It simply gives the trader time to review the market situation, limit drawdown and change tactics. Also, if the drawdown is greater than 15%, the lock-in may give the trader false hope of a good outcome if trading remains piecemeal.

Example 3

Let's imagine we are trading the EUR/USD pair; the deposit size is $3,000. We opened ourselves to buying trades that turned out to be losses. Both were 0.3 lots in size, the loss in the first case was $300, while in the second case it was $150. Thus, we have $2,550 left for future trades.

In this situation, we can open 2 block trades with the same volumes as before or 1 lot of 0.6 trade size. If we only close the losing trades, the drawdown will be $450, however the psychological pressure will not allow us to do so. An inexperienced trader turns to a more experienced trader for help. The latter recommends simply closing the floating loss and restoring the account size with a series of subsequent trades.

However, they might recommend parallel trading with smaller volumes.

A new series of trades will be based on the initial trading system if it has previously yielded positive results or it will be based on some new approaches. However, the work will be done for smaller volumes, say, 0.1 lot and the Take Profit target levels will be more humble: not a 100 but, say, 30 points. So, if we trade 0.1 lots and win 30 points on each trade, we will need 15 profitable trades to cover the $450 loss. Of course, in this case, we will need more time than we expected, but this is not so relevant if we succeed in restoring the account.

The Martingale method suggests opening a duplicate trade in the opposite direction. In the example above, we should have locked in the $300 loss and opened a 0.6 lot with the goal of making a 100-point profit. If all goes well, our profit would be $600, and after deducting the previous loss, we would make $300 net profit.

As you may have noticed, blocking gives you time to review your decisions, while the Martingale method helps offset losses aggressively. However, you must remember that it increases the risk of losing even more. It's up to you to decide if the loss is worth risking.

A Drawdown is unpleasant, but you will be fine if you don't let it get too deep. If you are already on a drawdown, you should do the following:

- If you are using a reliable strategy that has made profits many times, you should simply block the losses and continue trading with the same strategy but with a smoother money management system.
- If you doubt the effectiveness of your strategy, block losses and find a new one.

As long as there are no set ways to escape a drawdown, you will just have to keep trading. You need to find the weak points in your strategy and try to fix them. Reviewing your risk and money management rules will also be efficient. Be disciplined, stick to money management rules, trade systematically and drawdowns won't become a problem.

Market Movements

Most of the traders I have met absolutely want to conquer the market. Some are successful, but only occasionally, failing to turn this conquest into a permanent victory. The reasons are many, from insufficient skills or experience to a lack of the holy grail, with insufficient money reason somewhere in between. Well, quite a set of excuses. However, these reasons are somewhat true as all traders are different and use their trading potential differently.

Two Important Trader Opinions

There are two main opinions in the market that divide all traders. The first are the stochastics, those who want to predict price movements. The second, the agnostics, are moving with the market, constantly watching it. The former are an overwhelming minority, while the latter make up around 90%. And even if you are a stochastic, chances are you are also a bit of an agnostic.

What makes traders choose one way or another? Again, the reasons are many, but first and foremost, people tend to back up their opinions with theories, whether scientific or not.

The Effective Theory of the Market

Effective market theory, for example, tells us that all market players have access to the same information that enables them to analyze and predict market movements. In this way, each new piece of information already has a price in the market. All market players act rationally, like robots, to make the most of it, while a single trader cannot influence the market.

However, this has nothing to do with reality. What about legal action involving traders who used insider tips to speculate in the markets? Or how about those who buy a certain coin to increase demand? That's it. Theories work for ideal markets, not real ones.

Reasons for Market Movements

Any movement that occurs in a real market has a mix of reasons behind it; at any given time, those ratios may be different, and the correlation between them may also be different. The point to understand is that no emotion, speech or data release can influence the price without someone actually placing an order to buy or sell. If a bullish candlestick is going up, this means that people are pressing the Buy button again and again, even with the selling price increasing,

And the same goes for a bearish candlestick. These are the basics of price movement mechanics. Why then do mass buying and mass selling occur? Effective market theory has an answer ready for us again. A trader will sell the assets of a country in case the local key interest rate falls, unemployment rises, war conflict breaks out, etc. In other words, if a trader understands that an asset is at risk, they will try to get rid of it as soon as possible, even if the price is not so good.

Conversely, if the key interest rate is rising or say, a QE program is coming to an end, a trader will buy the appropriate assets. However, you understand, of course, that any market has trends, both short-term, medium-term and long-term, each influenced by various factors and with different weights. Before reversing a long-term trend, the short-term trend should fade first. Furthermore, any market has all kinds of traders: large, medium and small, and all of them operate at different levels in different time periods.

Breaking down all the political and economic factors, traders who see a bearish candle have to ask themselves one question: is anyone selling, who is buying from them? There are some hidden reasons that make people buy while the market is down. Those reasons, however, are primarily emotional in nature. Many people underestimate the emotional factor and trading psychology and yet the same people want to conquer the market or wait until the price reverses because 'it's going to be there, just allow it at some point. In many cases, it won't be there for long, and the trader will suffer catastrophic losses.

The market is simple and sophisticated. It is a chaos, but a self-regulated one. It is a paradox, a mixture of desires, fears and decisions, both considered and hasty. Every market move happens not for nothing, but the reasons are many, dynamic and ever changing. That is why predicting how long a movement will last or how long the price will correct is practically impossible.

CHAPTER 3

TRADING WITH TRENDLINES

Modern technical analysis uses trendlines. Many traders incorporate such lines into their trading strategies, using them not only on price charts but also on indicator charts. We can say that a trend line is one of the simplest instruments used for chart analysis. At the same time, regardless of its simplicity, this instrument is highly efficient.

Trend lines can show where to enter in the direction of the trend and where the current trend could end. The analysis of the price chart itself is a nice bonus - there is an opinion that the indicator signals are lagging, and it is the price that is of particular importance. However, we must keep in mind that all trading options must be customized, and various ways of using both graphical analysis tools and indicator signals must be tested.

Rising Trend Line

An ascending trendline is a line drawn from left to right through the lows. The second minimum must be higher than the first. To draw the line, two points are enough.

Many authors point to the third point as confirmation that the trend line has been drawn correctly. However, the moment the price touches the line, many traders try to buy now, without waiting for confirmation. As a general rule, buying on a trend line bounce always occurs with a small Stop Loss, so the risk is not that high. This is why most traders neglect confirmation a bit.

As an example, let's look at the trend line on the EUR/JPY chart above. To draw it, we take two marginal minima and draw a line through them. It is important to extend the line to the right so that we can see when to test this line for price. In our example, at the moment of testing the trend line, the price bounces back and continues to move up. We can say that the uptrend continues until the trend line is broken.

Downtrend

A descending trend line is drawn through the highs. To draw it, we need two points on the chart, the second is lower than the first.

Here, we must also remember that it is advisable to wait for the third line to form and confirm that the descending trend line has been drawn correctly. Anyway, we must remember that drawing trend lines is an art and therefore subjective. That is why different traders can draw different lines that are important to them. The more experienced the trader, the better they draw the lines.

As an example, let's take the latest chart of the AUD/USD pair. As we can see, a downward trend is developing. To draw the trend line, we take two marginal highs and try to extend the line as far as possible. At the time of testing, the price bounces back and continues to decline. Also, after the third test, the fourth occurred, after which the prices bounced back down.

How to Use Trend Lines

The easiest option is to trade rebounds off the trend line. In our example of an ascending trend line on the Brent chart, you can open a buy trade at the price of approximately 61.60 at the time of the fifth test. Place a Stop Loss below 60.00. As for the Take Profit, place it above the previous high because the trend is up and the price is likely to continue to rise.

Alternatively, we can do it without placing a TP, by moving our SL after the price. With such a strategy, we do not limit profits, we let it grow, which is recommended by many experts in technical analysis.

In the AUD/USD pair example, we should consider a sell trade at the time of another trend line test. We can say that in this case, the trend line acts as the resistance line. A sell trade could open at 0.6745, the SL is then placed above 0.6760.

We can expect a breakout of the nearest low here. That is why the TP is placed at 0.6630 or moves the SL after the price chart. If the buyers manage to push the price above the trendline, we should consider the end of the current trend and a possible trend reversal to the upside.

It should be noted that this is the simplest option of trading with the trend line but at the same time, the most efficient because the trader enters the market at the time of the development of the correction, and it is very likely that we will get the best price on it.

Channel Line

Many traders add a channel line to the trend line. Such a line is drawn parallel to the trend line. It is believed that the price will move within the channel for some time until it breaks its upper or lower border; after that, the channel line can be redrawn.

If we are talking about an ascending channel, we should buy from the lower border of the channel and close the trade near its upper border. We can also try to sell from the upper border. However, it is important to realize that in such a case, we will be trading against the trend, we risk seeing a break of the channel border and strong growth in the direction of the trend breaking off.

In the example with the gold price chart, we see prices bouncing off the upper border of the channel and heading to test the lower border, from which they bounce up. With the breakout of the lower border of the channel, the trend changes to a bottom.

However, there is a trick here. As a general rule, prices can go from the breakout point to the width of the channel. Also, if the upper border of the channel breaks up, this can be interpreted as a strong signal of the trend continuation. And if the prices, as in our example, have broken the channel to the downside, this is a weak signal, because the trend is reversed here.

In the example with the descending AUD/USD channel, we also see a bounce at the lower edge of the channel and price growth at its upper edge. We drew such a channel beforehand and got the last two signals after drawing it. Currently, prices remain within the channel, and the decline will most likely continue after another test of the upper border of this channel. If prices break out, we can talk about a change from the current trend to an uptrend.

Trend Line Breakout

Trend lines behave like horizontal support and resistance levels: at the moment of a breakout, they simply swap places. The same with the trend lines: if the price is above the line, this line is the support. If the price is below the trend line, the latter acts as the resistance line.

In the example with the AUD/USD chart, we see a strong uptrend. The prices push the rising trend line and at a certain point, this line is broken. However, we should not rush to sell, we should wait for the prices to go back to the broken trend line and enter the sell trade only after that. The SL, in this case, is placed above the trend line or behind the local high. The TP can be placed at the closest support level, or we can simply follow the chart, moving the SL. In our case, the support and resistance lines have changed places.

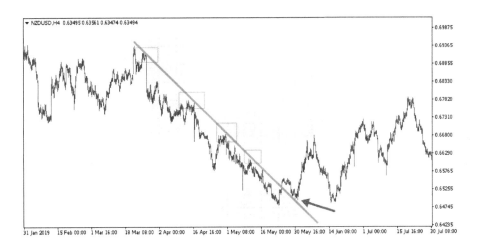

In the example below with NZD/USD, we see prices, after a breakout of the descending trend line, we test it from above and only then go higher. In this case, we can also wait for the price to return to the dashed line and only after that we consider entering a buy trade.

CHAPTER 4

TRADING CHART PATTERNS

A pattern is a repeated element in various aspects of life, such as nature, psychology, music, design, trading, and so on. A pattern in trading is a consistent and repeated combination of data on prices, volumes, or indicators.

What is a Chart Pattern?

Chart patterns are specific and repeated areas on price charts that are also known as price patterns or formations.

Over the years of monitoring financial markets, it was discovered that the price charts occasionally displayed chart patterns (or price patterns) that could be used to predict future movements. There are formations that show the continuation of tendencies and patterns that show their reversal. It is important to note that the formation of price patterns on charts does not guarantee that the price will move in the direction predicted by the patterns, but there is a possibility of matching and may aid in trading.

Head & Shoulders and Inverted Head & Shoulders Chart Patterns

These are reversal patterns that typically form at the price chart's local lows and highs in either an ascending or descending trend. The patterns indicate that the current trend is weakening and that the price will either begin a correction or reverse the trend to the opposite side.

Head & Shoulders

The Head and Shoulders chart pattern is formed at highs in an ascending trend. A neckline is drawn between 1 and 2. Only after the price settles below the neckline is the chart pattern considered fully formed. Following that, the price is expected to fall by at least the pattern height, which is measured in pips from the pattern's high to the neckline. It is advised to sell immediately after the price breaks the neckline or to wait until it retraces to the line after breaking it.

Inverted Head & Shoulders

At lows in a descending trend, an inverted head and shoulders chart pattern forms. A bottom line is drawn between 1 and 2 (neckline). Only after the price has fixed above the bottom line is the chart pattern considered fully formed. Following that, the price is expected to rise by at least the pattern height, which is measured in pips from the pattern's low to the neckline. It is advised to buy when the price breaks the bottom line or to wait until the price returns to the line after breaking it.

How to Trade the Head and Shoulders Pattern

The Head and Shoulders pattern is a classic pattern of technical analysis tools. Let's take a look at its main elements, as well as the features of trading it.

What's The Head and Shoulders pattern once again?

First of all, it is worth remembering that this pattern forms at the end of an uptrend and signals a possible reversal. I say possible because Forex is unpredictable, as is any financial market, and it would be the least bit unwise to insist that the formation pattern is necessarily Head and Shoulders and that the market will soon reverse.

In the market, you can never be sure of interpreting things correctly. However, the formation chart pattern will allow you to make an assumption about the next move and in the presence of certain conditions, enter the trade in the chosen direction.

Keep in mind that the longer the time period in which the pattern has formed, the more important the pattern will be. To understand how the Head and Shoulders pattern is formed, let's see the pattern:

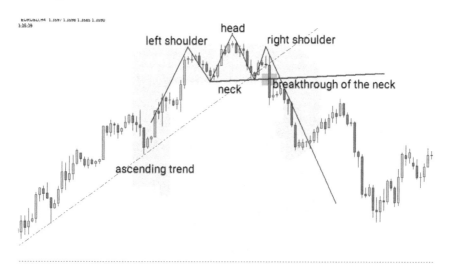

After an uptrend on the EUR/USD chart, the pattern in question formed on H4. To make it clearer, I have marked the pattern formed by the right and left shoulders and the head, the latter being the tallest of the three peaks. It is worth noting that the right shoulder is lower than the left, thus increasing the importance of the whole pattern. Shoulders are not always symmetrical and can have their lows at different levels. There are formations with announcements of almost horizontal necks and with inclinations.

Along the lows of the shoulders, you can trace the neckline, which is in fact, the support level. A breakthrough of this same line is considered a sell signal.

In addition to this, the important parameters of the pattern, according to classical technical analysis, are the following:

- Trading volumes rising after a breakthrough at the neckline.
- The target level.
- Use of the support line (the neckline) as resistance.

We will discuss all the parameters in more detail later.

When to enter the trade and where to Place a Stop Loss?

One can enter the trade through this pattern in various ways:

1. Place a pending Sell Stop order below the neckline or enter the market, if you are on the computer, after the next advance. The drawback here is that you can enter the market with a false advance, in which case the price will spike and go higher, canceling the Head and Shoulders pattern. Such a hasty entry into the market carries great risk, but allows you to enter the market at the best price.

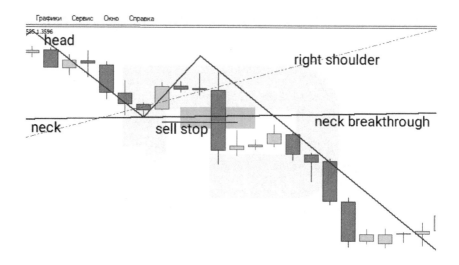

2. Enter the market at the neckline test from below, in other words, at the moment when support turns into resistance.

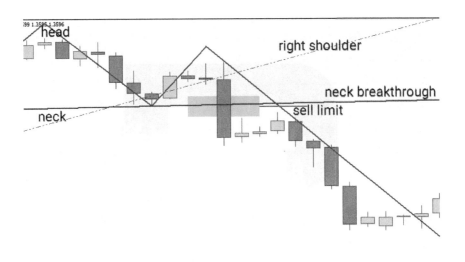

After the break, when the candlestick closes below the neckline, you can either place a Sell Limit order or continue to monitor the situation and enter the market position. The advantage of such an entry is your confidence in the advance. The drawback is that the price does not always reach the neckline or does not return for the test, while the break is followed by a strong move with virtually no retracement. In our example, the price would not get to the limit order.

3. The most conservative entry is selling after the break of the recent low, which emerges after the break of the neckline.

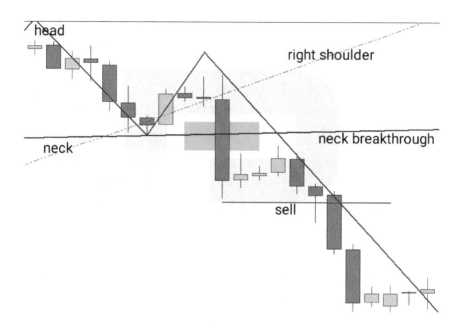

The drawback of this approach is the fact that a fairly large part of the movement is lost and a lot of risk is involved in the trade, because the Stop Loss will be in the same place as in the previous two cases, while the potential target will be closer to the entry point.

The biggest mistake beginners make, trading the Head and Shoulders pattern, is too hasty entry. Traders try to enter the market before the neckline break. But remember that until the neck is broken, the pattern is not considered complete, so always start acting after the break.

Also, you can use indicators (such as the MACD) to spot the divergence between the peak of the left shoulder and the head, which confirms the expected price reversal.

Stop losses are usually placed below the peak of the right shoulder. An option of the third type of market entry will be to place the Stop Loss above the neckline, that is, the current resistance level. This will help minimize risks, although it must comply with the current market situation (for example, executed by measuring the distance that the price has covered after the break).

Trading Volumes

According to classical technical analysis and the interpretation of the head and shoulders pattern, an important parameter is an increase in trading volume at the break of the neckline. This means that traders widen their positions, implying a further decline in price, thus confirming the entry along the pattern.

When the price moves from the left shoulder to the head, the volumes are also reduced. Conversely, a drop in price from the peak of the head to the base of the right shoulder leads to increased volumes. However, it is worth remembering that this rule cannot be used in Forex as there is no indication of volume as it is there. Therefore, the information can be used in other trading platforms, where the trader has access to this data, such as in futures and stock markets.

How to Calculate the Target Level of the Head & Shoulders Pattern?

The target in the Head and Shoulders pattern, i.e. the point where Take Profit will be placed, is calculated as the distance from the peak of the head to the neckline, drawn from the breakout point. In our example, this distance is 136 pips.

Keep in mind that it is a design value, so other factors that hinder price movement, such as strong resistance lines on the way, must also be taken into account. In these cases, the position can be closed when the price reaches a significant level, or a part of the position can be closed, and the other part is left to run.

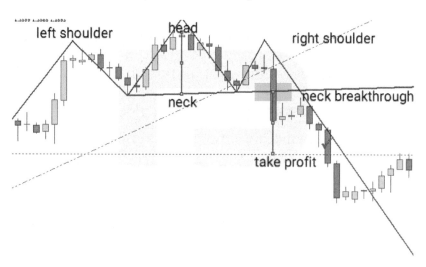

Along with the pattern indicating a reversal in the uptrend, its mirror image, the inverted head and shoulders, is considered. It has the same parameters and market entry conditions, the only difference is that it is formed at the end of a downtrend and means price growth. On the xhart, it looks like this:

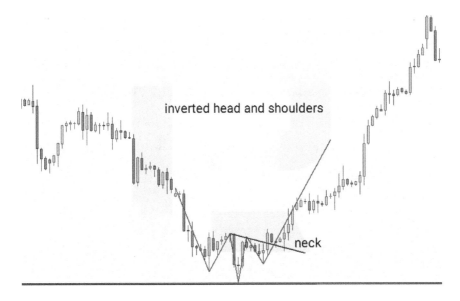

inverted head and shoulders

neck

In conclusion, Last but not least, it should be noted that beginner traders often see the Head and Shoulders pattern, even though it is not there, just because they want to see it. Don't look for trend figures where there aren't any. Don't make them up. No one doubts the power of your imagination.

Double Top & Double Bottom Chart Patterns

These are reversal chart patterns that typically form at the price chart's local lows and highs in either an ascending or descending trend. The patterns indicate that the current trend is weakening and that the price will either begin a correction or reverse the trend to the opposite side.

Double Top

A double top chart pattern forms at highs in an ascending trend. A horizontal bottom line is drawn across 1. Only after the price settles below the bottom line is the chart pattern considered fully formed. The price is then expected to fall by at least the pattern height, which is measured in pips from the pattern's highs to the bottom line. It is advised to sell immediately after the price breaks the neckline or to wait until it returns to the line after breaking it.

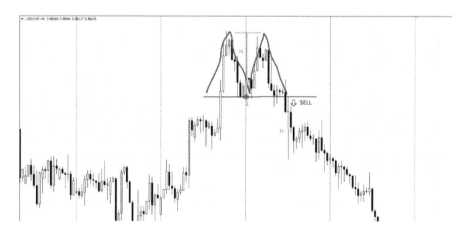

Double Bottom

The Double Bottom chart pattern appears at lows in a descending trend. A horizontal neckline is drawn across 1. Only after the price has fixed above the neckline is the chart pattern considered fully formed. Following that, the price is expected to rise by at least the pattern height, which is measured in pips from the pattern's lows to the bottom line. It is advised to buy when the price breaks the neckline or to wait until the price returns to the line (retracement) after breaking it.

Triple Top & Triple Bottom Patterns

These are reversal chart patterns that typically form at the price chart's local lows and highs in either an ascending or descending trend. The patterns indicate that the current trend is weakening and that the price will either begin a correction or reverse the trend to the opposite side.

Triple Top

The Triple Top chart pattern forms at highs in an ascending trend. A horizontal neckline is drawn across 1 and 2. Only after the price settles below the neckline is the chart pattern considered fully formed. The price is then expected to fall by at least the pattern height, which is measured in pips from the pattern's highs to the bottom line. It is advised to sell immediately after the price breaks the neckline or to wait until it returns to the line after breaking it.

Triple Bottom

The Triple Bottom chart pattern forms at lows in a descending trend. 1 and 2 are connected by a neckline. Only after the price has fixed above the neckline is the chart pattern considered fully formed. Following that, the price is expected to rise by at least the pattern height, which is measured in pips from the pattern's lows to the bottom line. It is advised to buy when the price breaks the bottom line or to wait until the price returns to the line after breaking it.

How to Trade the Double & Triple Top, Double & Triple Bottom Patterns

In this section we will discuss how to trade popular and quite widespread chart analysis patterns Double Top, Triple Top and its opposite Double Bottom, Triple Bottom.

As we can tell from the name, these patterns form at the top or bottom of a trend. Meanwhile, the data shows that they can be found on all timeframes and chart types (Japanese candlesticks, bars, line charts). The only difference in timing is the time it takes for the pattern to form and the time it takes for the signal to settle.

These patterns belong to the reversal category. This means that signal work usually leads to a reversal of the current trend or at least a deep price correction. Now let's talk about these pattern technical analysis tools more scrupulously and learn how to use them in trading.

Formation Rules of the Patterns

Let's start with the principles of pattern formation.

Double Top

Typically, a double top forms at the apex of an uptrend. The longer the timeframe, the more reliable the pattern (this is relevant to all patterns discussed in this section). At the same time, the signal can work in any time frame, including M1, M5, etc.

A double top pattern looks like 2 tops that formed successively. Theoretically, buyers drive the price higher, and then a part of them begins to lock their positions, thus lowering the quotes. At this time, some newcomers step in, raising the price to the same level.

The two peaks do not need to be the same, point to point, but they should resemble the two tops of the mountains. Then the first buyers start taking profits, the price starts to decline, and the second wave has nothing to do but close positions with a minimal loss or profit.

As a result, the quotes fall and the real trend changes direction. The support level in this case is the low formed between the two bottoms. This is the starting point for trading and determining the trade's potential. We will talk about entry points a bit later.

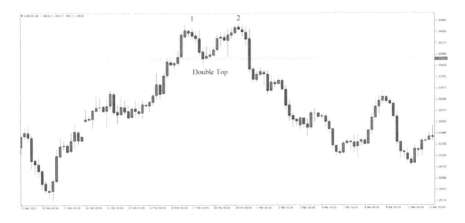

Triple Top

A Triple Top is a slightly tweaked Double Top. In practice, it forms as follows: After the first two tops are formed, another group of buyers enters the market in the hope of further price growth. In fact, at that moment the quotes rise to a maximum and may even renew the previous highs, but this is it.

The first wave of buyers has a larger critical mass (has more open buy positions), due to which the quotes begin to decline at the closing of positions, test the support level, then form a downtrend after breaking the uptrend. Looking at the charts in history, we can see that this does not necessarily happen, and the trend can reverse without special patterns.

Double Bottom

A double bottom reflects the top double mirror. It looks like two back lows with a small gap in the middle. It works out like this: sellers rule the market and push the price down, but when it hits the bottom, some sellers from the first wave close their remaining positions, and prices start to move up.

In this case, the resistance level is the high between the two lows. Upon reaching the resistance level, the price breaks away from it and the trend changes direction. The first stream of sellers take profit, and the second wave, realizing they had been tricked, closed positions at a loss. Thus, the citations begin to grow almost immediately.

Triple Bottom

The Triple Bottom is somewhat shaped, similar to the Triple Top. Following the formation of the first lower, a new group of sellers attempts to profit from the decline, but their trading volume is insufficient, and the price begins to rise.

When the price reaches the resistance level, the second and third wave traders usually take a loss on their open positions, and they have nothing to do but close them. As a result, the quotes test the resistance level, start to rise and change the trend.

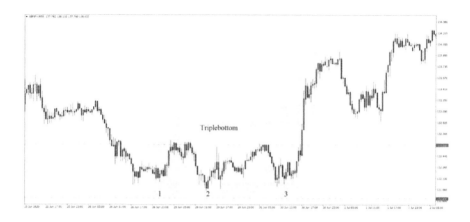

How to Trade Double Top and Bottom Chart Patterns?

All that remains is to interpret the trade input for these patterns.

Double Top

As long as the pattern signifies a reversal of the uptrend, we will open short trades. Aggressive traders can open positions on the formation of the second top, which in my opinion is not always wise as it is risky.

Conservative trading is a more suitable option. We sell after the price breaks the support level; it will be perfect if the price closes below this level. In this case, the pattern will most likely start to work, and there will be no third wave of buyers.

Place a stop loss behind the high pattern. Of course, it turns out to be quite large and in certain cases, it goes against the rules of money management. If so, refrain from trading with this group of patterns.

The potential profit is calculated as the distance between the support and high levels and is equal to the potential Take Profit. Ideally use 60-80% of the pattern height.

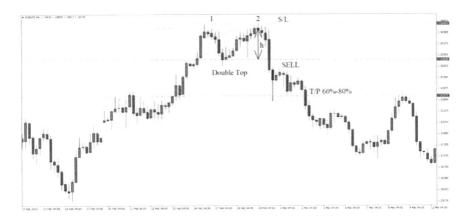

Double Bottom

Open buy trades as long as the Double Bottom forms at the bottom of a downtrend. The algorithm is as follows: open a buy trade after the price reaches the resistance level for the second time (ideally, the candlestick closes above it).

Set a Stop Loss below the high and calculate the Take Profit based on the height of the pattern. As with Double Top, it features 60 to 80% of the pattern.

How to trade Triple Top and Bottom patterns?

Triple Top

A Triple Top is traded like a Double Top with the only difference being that the trade is entered after the third top is formed and the price reaches the support level. Calculate the Stop Loss and Take Profit as for a Double Top.

Triple Bottom

In the case of a triple bottom, the entry point will be at the breakout of the resistance level. After the candle closes above the resistance level, open the position. The SL and TP work in the same way as the double bottom.

Double/triple tops and bottoms are rare on charts. However, they can help an experienced trader make a good profit. Before you begin trading these patterns, carefully examine the charts and pattern formation conditions.

The principle will always be the same, but the patterns will vary slightly depending on the instrument. When choosing a time frame for trading, make sure the SL is not against your money management rules.

Wedge Chart Pattern

Wedge chart pattern is a reversal chart pattern formed by the highs and lows of two convergent lines, support and resistance. The chart pattern shares some characteristics with Triangle, with the main difference being a skew angle (of both lines forming it) in the same direction. When the price exits the chart pattern in the opposite direction of the skew, the wedge is considered broken. If the Wedge is formed at highs in an ascending trend, it is recommended to sell after the price settles below the support line; the chart pattern's target is the value of the chart pattern's base (H) in pips.

If a Wedge is formed at the lows of a descending trend, it is recommended to buy after the price settles above the resistance line; the chart pattern's target is the value of the chart pattern's base (H) in pips.

Triangle Chart Pattern

Triangle chart patterns are classified into three types:

Symmetrical Triangle

Symmetrical Triangle is a universal chart pattern that can forecast both a reversal and continuation of an existing trend. It is formed by the intersection of two convergent lines, support and resistance. If the price fixes above the resistance line, buy; if it fixes below the support line, sell. The chart pattern's target is the value of the pattern's base (H) in pips.

Ascending Triangle

The Ascending Triangle chart pattern is formed by a horizontal resistance line intersected by an ascending support line. After the price has stabilized above the resistance line, it is recommended to buy; the chart pattern's target is the value of the chart pattern's base (H) in pips.

Descending Triangle

A Descending Triangle is a chart pattern that forms between a horizontal support line and a descending resistance line. After the price settles below the support line, it is advised to sell; the chart pattern's target is the length of the chart pattern's base (H) in pips.

How to Trade the Wedge and Triangle Patterns

The Triangle Pattern appears on different charts quite often. The classic technical analysis tools consider it a pattern which means the continuation of the trend. However, in my opinion, this pattern can equally work in line with or against the existing trend.

Description of the Triangle Pattern

There are several types of triangles, each with its own specific characteristics. On the chart, a Triangle is made up of converging (less often diverging) lines of support and resistance. To draw a triangle, four points must be plotted on the chart, which are two back highs and two back lows; through these points, the sides of the Triangle (the support and resistance lines) are drawn.

As a rule, five waves form within the Triangle before it breaks. After the price breaks one side of the Triangle, a strong momentum (move) towards the breakout is likely to appear. It is similar to a spring that is squeezed deeper and deeper into the Triangle until it shoots up or down.

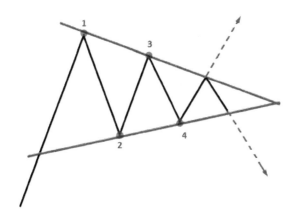

Types of the Triangle and its Execution

There are four types of triangles in technical analysis.

Equilateral or symmetrical triangle

A universal pattern that can continue the trend or go against it. It is formed by the converging lines of support and resistance. The following chart shows that the bears are gradually pushing the price down while the bulls are pushing it up from the support line. In the end, some of them get stronger, and the price breaks through the edge of the Symmetrical Triangle, gathering Stop Losses and pending orders on the way.

A position should be opened in the direction of the breakout after the price closes outside the Symmetrical Triangle boundaries. If the upper border is broken, we buy, placing a limiting Stop Loss at the nearest Triangle low; it is very likely that the execution will be the size of the base of the Triangle (the largest wave), let's call it H (the value in points). If the lower border of the Triangle is broken, we sell, placing a Stop Loss at the nearest high of the Triangle. The size of the pattern execution (the H value in points) will be the base of the triangle (the largest wave).

Ascending Triangle

This is the uptrend continuation chart pattern, although a reverse execution is sometimes possible. The ascending triangle forms between the ascending support line and the horizontal resistance level. In the uptrend, the bulls run into a strong resistance level that they fail to overcome immediately. Price pullbacks downward from this level, forming the waves of the ascending triangle. Gradually, they get weaker and at some point the bulls, having bought all the bearish sell orders, break this level up, accumulating Stop Losses and pending buy orders.

On a breakout of the upper border of the ascending triangle, it is recommended to buy. The Stop Loss is placed below the nearest low of the Triangle, the execution is the size of the base of the Triangle H (in points), which is the largest wave.

Descending Triangle

This is the chart pattern that continues a downtrend, although it can sometimes run against the trend. The descending resistance line and the horizontal support level form it. In a downtrend, bears run into a strong support level, which they fail to break through immediately. Several pullbacks then follow from this level upwards, forming the Descending Triangle. In the end, the bears sweep all the buy orders from the bulls and break the support level from top to bottom, picking up Stop Losses and pending sell orders. After breaking the lower border of the Descending Triangle, it is recommended to sell; Stop Loss is placed above the nearest high of the Triangle. The size of the run (H) is the size of the base of the triangle, which is its largest wave.

Diverging Triangle

This chart pattern is the opposite of the symmetrical triangle; it can indicate the end of the current trend or vice versa, demonstrate a correction, after which the trend will resume. It is formed by the divergent lines of support and resistance. The angle is looking to the left. The pattern trades the same as the Converging Triangles. In my opinion, it is not really smart to trade it on the border breakout as the latter occurs at the base of the Triangle after the biggest wave, and a technically correct Stop Loss for the closest high/low will be too big, stop/profit ratio will almost be 1:1.

Therefore, a position must be entered after breakout. If we expect price rise, we must enter the rebound from the support line; if we are expecting a decline, then after a bounce off the resistance line. In this case, the stop / profit ratio will be comfortable because the Stop Loss at the nearest minimum / maximum will be small while the execution (profit) - much larger, at least it extends to the opposite edge of the Diverging Triangle, and if breaks through, as big as the last biggest wave in the Triangle (base) too.

Description and Execution of the Wedge Pattern

Typically, the wedge is considered a reversal pattern, which forms at the highs and lows of a price chart in an uptrend or downtrend. A wedge is quite similar to a triangle, forming between the two converging lines of support and resistance. The main difference between the two patterns is the slope of the two lines and the pattern itself: all the lines are sloped up or down. According to the inclination of the sides, the wedge can be of two types: ascending and descending.

Rising Wedge

It is formed by the two converging and rising lines of support and resistance. If the rising wedge forms at the highs of a price chart in an uptrend, it indicates a likely reversal or correction. On a breakout of the lower edge of the Wedge, it is recommended to sell with a Stop Loss above the nearest high of the Wedge and execution sized as the H base (the largest wave at the base of the pattern).

If a rising wedge forms in a downtrend after renewal of the lows, it signifies a correction, and should the lower border of the pattern break through the downtrend, a continuation is likely. After a breakout of the lower selling edge of the Wedge is recommended, a Stop Loss is placed above the nearest high, the execution is sized as the H base of the Wedge (the largest wave at the base of the pattern).

Falling Wedge

This wedge pattern is formed by the two converging and descending lines of support and resistance. If a falling wedge forms at the lows of a price chart in a downtrend, it means a possible correction or even a reversal. In case the upper border of the pattern (the resistance line) is broken, it is recommended to buy, with a Stop Loss below the nearest low. A gain is blocked after growth to the size of the base H (the largest wave at the base of the pattern).

If a falling wedge forms after renewing the highs in an uptrend, it may indicate a continuation of the trend. In this case, a falling wedge is a correction after growth. In case the upper border is broken, it is recommended to buy, with a Stop Loss below the nearest low of the pattern. The run is expected to be at least the size of the base H (the largest wave at the base of the pattern).

Triangle and wedge chart technical analysis patterns are quite frequent to appear on charts and can be quite helpful in assessing the outlook for future price movements. The probability of its execution seems to me quite high, and it is worth including it in the portfolio. It just takes practice to find patterns on the price chart and react to all the other factors like the current trend, stop/profit ratio and fundamental factors.

Diamond Chart Pattern

A Diamond reversal chart pattern is extremely rare. It is formed at the price chart's local highs and lows in either an ascending or descending trend. The chart patterns indicate that the current trend is weakening and that the price will either begin a correction or reverse the trend to the opposite side.

If the Diamond pattern forms at highs in an ascending trend, it is recommended to sell after the price settles below the support line; the chart pattern's height (H) in pips is the target. If a Diamond is formed at lows in a descending trend, it is recommended to buy after the price fixes above the resistance line; the chart pattern's height (H) in pips is the target.

How to Trade Diamond Chart Pattern

Trading Reversal Chart Formations

Today we will learn how to trade a chart pattern called diamond. Compared to other patterns, the Diamond pattern appears very rarely on the chart. This is the number one reason why it is unpopular with most traders. In lower timeframes, the diamond takes a short time to form and could work as a signal for a couple of candles. On higher timeframes, from D1 and above, the pattern can take months to form, which does not enhance its attractiveness to traders.

Not all traders can afford to wait two or three months for the signal to form. However, the Diamond has its advantages: it almost always works with the signal and can generate substantial profits.

Conditions and Principles of the Formation of the Diamond Chart Pattern

The diamond is a reversal pattern that forms at the top of an uptrend or the bottom of a downtrend. It is easy to tell that it looks like a diamond.

Diamond Pattern that Forms at the Top of a Trend

The formation at the top of the trend occurs as follows. First, the price forms an expanding triangle. It can be isosceles or slightly irregular in shape. After the price reaches the highs, it begins to fade, and on the chart, the amplitude of the price fluctuations decreases. This is a decrease in volatility in a sense, when most of the traders in the market, especially the bigger ones, have taken their positions and start to wait for other traders to act.

Then the second wave of traders enters the scene – they have noticed the pattern and are eager to make money on the signal. The point is that the Diamond pattern solution is based on the greed of newcomers to the market. However, they cannot compete with the first wave of traders and simply buy where the first wave traders start to sell (closing positions that have already generated some profit).

As a result, the prices begin to decline rapidly, generating some panic in the market, so the second wave of buyers also rush to close their positions. Therefore, the diamond shape forms at the top of the uptrend.

Diamond

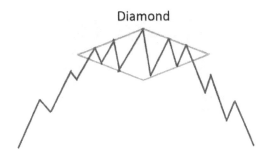

Diamond Chart Pattern that Forms at the Bottom of a Trend

A similar situation can be seen at the lows of a downtrend, only market participants swap places. For a while, the market is dominated by bears causing a downtrend. At a certain point, the price starts a sideways movement, expanding the amplitude (creating an expanding triangle), then the volatility reduces and a second converging triangle forms on the chart.

Then market participants see the Diamond, and their greed overwhelms them. They begin to sell actively, but in general, sellers are less than those who take the profit from the first wave (the profit is made by a reverse buy order). As a result, quotes begin to grow.

Then the greed of the second wave of traders plays an evil joke on them, and the closing of their losing positions leads to strong price growth. The first wave of sellers closes their positions with a profit, and the second with a loss. In general, no matter how often or rarely the Diamond chart pattern forms, there will always be those who were late to the first wave, and their greed and lack of experience lead to the work of the pattern.

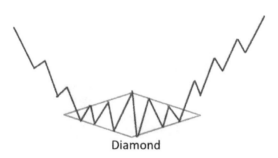
Diamond

In some cases, when the critical mass of the second wave exceeds the first wave, the Diamond pattern can turn into a continuation trading pattern. However, this situation is not a solution of the pattern and is best left out.

Opening a Sell Position with the Diamond Chart pattern

Once the pattern is completed on the line chart, it should look like a diamond. The price explodes in the lower right corner (support line); the candlestick should close below this line.

Open a sell trade with your preferred volume. Place a stop loss above the nearest high. Normally, this is the upper right corner resistance line, near which the price closed. The potential benefit is calculated as 60-80% of the diamond height (vertical dimension).

Alternatively, you can enter the trade on a breakout of Diamond's low. This is a more conservative way of opening a position, which, in some cases, can protect the trader from a false pattern breakout. The potential profit is calculated in the same way, as 60-80% of the height of Diamond. A SL can be placed as described above or above the height of the Diamond.

Open a Buy Trade with the Diamonds Chart Patterns

The price breaks the upper right resistance line, and the candle closes above this line. Open a buy order with your preferred volume. Place n SL below the nearest low, which is normally the lower right support line near which the candle closed. The potential profit is also calculated as 60-80% of the Diamond chart pattern size.

Alternatively, you can enter the trade on a breakout of the height of the Diamond. As with the sell trade, this is a more conservative option. A SL is placed below the nearest low as above or below the Diamond low.

Closing thoughts

There are several occasions in which you should not open trades:

- The pattern is not complete.
- No trading inside the Diamond Formation chart pattern

Always follow your risk management rules when entering a trade. As long as the Diamond chart pattern forms on higher timeframes, the size of the SL may be too large at times, however, you may open a trade at the beginning of a trade. Regardless of whether the Diamond pattern is rare on the chart, you can use it quite successfully.

Rectangle Chart Pattern

The rectangle chart pattern is a universal chart pattern that can predict both a reversal and continuation of an existing trend. The price appears to be consolidating in a sideways channel formed by horizontal support and resistance levels. If the price fixes above the resistance line, buy; if it fixes below the support line, sell. The chart pattern's height (H) in pips is the take profit of the pattern.

Flag Chart Pattern

A flag is a chart pattern that shows the continuation of an actual trend. The price is forming a correctional area (Cloth) after a strong price movement (Flagpole), which is either horizontal or sloping towards the Flagpole. The Cloth can be in the shape of a

Rectangle, Triangle, or Wedge. It is recommended to buy once the price has completed the correction and is above the Cloth's resistance line. The height of the Flagpole is the pattern's target.

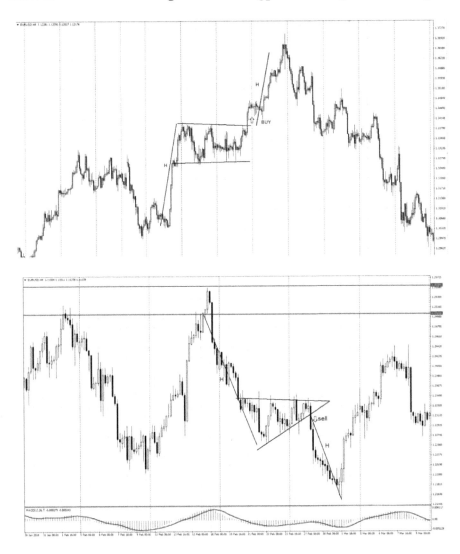

How to Trade Flag and Pennant Patterns

The flag and Pennant appear quite often on price charts. They are trend continuation patterns, which work in the presence of a strong trend, just like trend reversal patterns. When such patterns appear, we can forecast that the trend will continue. If a flag or a pennant forms in an uptrend, this means that the bulls are controlling the market, and after a small downward correction, in which the patterns form, the prices could continue to grow. If a flag or pennant forms in a downtrend, this means that bears are still strong, and after a correction to the upside, in which patterns could form, price is likely to continue to decline.

Flag Pattern

It appears after a strong price push along with the existing trend. First comes the price push, called the flagpole. Next, a rectangular correction area is formed, bounded by parallel lines of support and resistance - this is the fabric of the Flag. An important detail here is that the fabric must be leaning against the previous push (the flagpole) or it can be oriented horizontally.

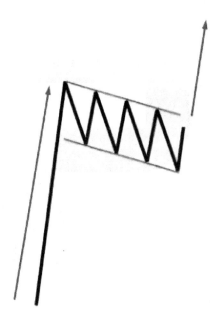

Pennant Pattern

Like the flag, the pattern emerges after a strong price push, which is called a pole. Then the correction area is formed, which looks like a small converging triangle or wedge. An important detail again: if the Pennant is formed by a converging Triangle, it can be of any type (symmetrical, ascending, descending), while if it is formed by a Wedge, it must be tilted against the impulse (the pole).

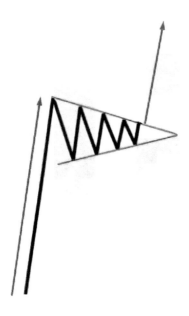

Flags

The pattern is a trend continuation pattern, so once it forms, the trend becomes the only option.

A Flag Form in an Uptrend

A flag formed in an uptrend is called a bull. After the appearance of an upward impulse (the flagpole), we must wait for the flag to form and break upwards. The criteria for the breakout is a full candlestick or most of a candlestick closing above the resistance line of the Flag. Buying is recommended either on the breakout or after a pullback to the top edge of the flag. A stop loss is placed below the nearest low of the Flag, while the Take Profit is the size of the flagpole H (in points).

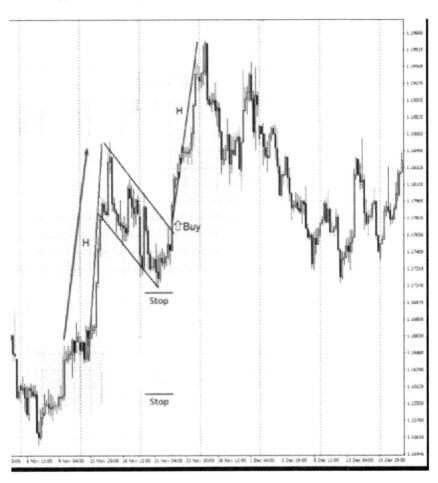

A Flag Form in a Downtrend

A flag emerging in a downtrend is called a bearish. After a downward momentum that constitutes the flagpole, we expect the flag pattern to form and break down. The criteria for the breakout will be a full candlestick or most of a candlestick closing below the support line of the flag. Selling is recommended either on the breakout or after a pullback to the lower edge of the flag. A Stop Loss is placed above the nearest high of the Flag, the profit is expected to be the size of the flagpole H (in points).

Pennants

The pennant, just like the flag, is a trend continuation pattern, so the trade must be in the trend only.

Pennant in an Uptrend

A pennant formed in an uptrend is called a bull. It gives a signal to buy after its upper border (the resistance line) breaks out. It is recommended to buy either at the breakout if for example, it is a strong movement after the publication of some news; or on a pullback to the broken resistance line. A SL is placed below the nearest minimum of the Pennant, a TP is estimated as the height of the H-post.

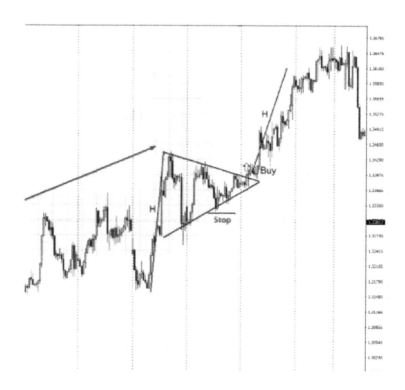

Pennant in a Downtrend

A pennant formed in a downtrend is called a bearish. It signals the sell after the lower border (the support level) breaks. It is recommended to sell either directly on the breakout, if it is for example, a strong move after the release of certain news, or after a pullback to the broken support line. A Stop Loss (SL) is placed below the nearest maximum of the Pennant, while a TP is estimated as the height of the H-post.

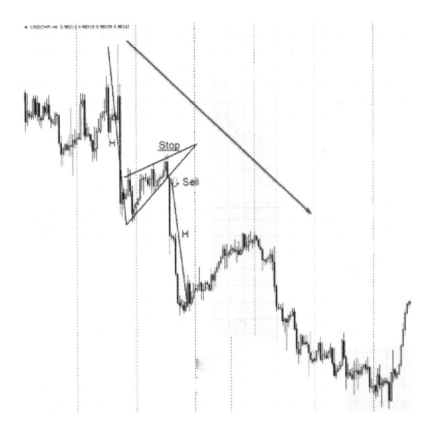

Among traders, the flag and pennant patterns are two of the most popular trend continuation patterns. They give a clear signal along with the current trend and most often provide an entry to a trade with a good stop/profit ratio of 1:2 or 1:3. The profit from executing these patterns is estimated as the size of the momentum (the pole) H, but important support/resistance levels should also be taken into account. It is better to secure a slightly smaller profit, approaching a strong level, and then lose everything if the price turns against the open position.

CHAPTER 5

SETTING STOP LOSS AND TAKE PROFIT

Stop Loss and Take Profit orders act like insurance, essentially being reverse orders. If for example, a pair was bought, when a Stop Loss or a Take Profit is triggered, a reverse (sell) trade is carried out, blocking the Profit (if the TP is triggered) or the Loss (if the TP is triggered).

What is Stop Loss and Take Profit?

A stop loss (SL) is a protection order that limits the trader's possible losses on an open position. When a certain level or amount of losses is reached, the trade is automatically closed. A Stop Loss is placed to limit losses or to retain profits. The order is placed in the profitable area in the latter case.

A Take Profit (TP) is an order that locks in profits without the involvement of the trader. The order automatically closes the trade when the price reaches a certain level.

Both Stop Loss and Take Profit must be placed in agreement with the party trader. For your trading to be stable and successful, these orders are mandatory. The Stop Loss minimizes losses and improves Systematic risk management.

Almost all trading strategies include the use of a Stop Loss and/or Take Profit. Each trader has their own money management (MM) criteria that tell them how much they can afford to lose on each trade. This is the strategy that indicates where to place a SL and a TP.

How to Place a Stop Loss

The trader defines how much they stand to lose, based on the MM, if something goes wrong. The strategy instructs them on where to place the Stop Loss.

Placing Take Profit and Stop Loss in a Pin Bar Strategy

The trader is using the Pin Bar strategy. At the top of an upward momentum, a Pin bar pattern has formed, and the trader plans to open a sell trade. In this case, a Stop Loss will be placed behind the maximum value of the candlestick signal. The milestone for a

Take Profit is the nearest support level. The possible profit / loss ratio in this case is 3: 1. In the first chart below, you can see where you should place the SL and TP depending on the trading strategy.

In the second chart, you see the result of the execution of the signal to sell.

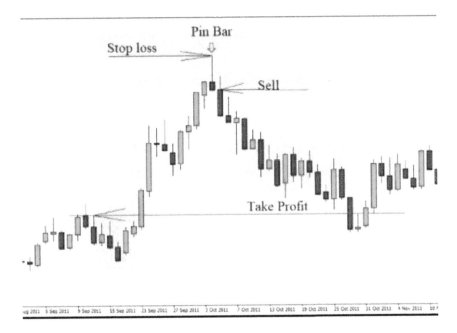

The Stop Loss is generally calculated in pips from the entry to the peak of the Pin Bar, accounting for the sum of the attainable losses, expressed in the basic currency of the deposit. The trader must first calculate the price of a point before placing the volume. For example, the Stop Loss is 40 pips, the available loss is 100 USD; 100 USD / 40 pips = the price of one pip is 2.25 USD. Therefore, the trade size is 0.25 lot.

With risk management, the trader can control the risks. For example, if they receive a signal with a win/loss ratio of 1 to 1, the trader should think twice before entering this trade. The ideal profit-to-loss ratio is at least 3 to 1.

Placing Take Profit and Stop Loss in a Pin Bar Strategy - 2

In the chart below, we can see a full Pin bar, and if we calculate the trade by the strategy, we will see that the closest support level is as far away as the Stop Loss, which gives a 1:1 ratio. So, we can filter this signal since it does not comply with the MM.

Placing Stop Loss on 2 MAs + Fractals

For the following example, let's take the simplest strategy based on two moving averages (MA) and fractals. The trader receives a signal to sell after the two MAs cross; then after a trade is opened, a Stop Loss is placed. The target milestone for the SL here is the fractal high (thus it can warrant trading false breakouts and moves). The trade should be closed at the time the MAs cross in the opposite direction. Provided that the place of the crossover is unknown at the time of opening the position, the trader must move the Stop Loss manually, keeping it at a certain distance from the price.

The distance is calculated based on several facts:

- The time frame in which the trade was entered.
- The volume of the open position.
- The risk the trader can afford in the trade.
- The volatility of the instrument (with highly volatile pairs, a small SL will simply close the position before the trader takes maximum profit).

If there are doubts that the price will be able to go in the necessary direction at least 3 times beyond the distance to the Stop Loss, it is better to skip such a trade. You should never place a lower SL than planned due to lack of funds or a desire to enter with higher volume, as this can lead to stupid losses. The trade can be closed preliminarily, before the price goes in the necessary direction.

Trailing Stop

I guess that many traders at least once found themselves in the situation when they opened a buy or sell position, placed the Take Profit 50-70 pips away from the entry point, and the Stop Loss - about 30-40 pips away and had to leave the workplace to attend to other matters. When they came back, they saw that price, missing the TP level by a couple of pips, had reversed, heading for the SL. Well, was it possible, if not avoidable, to optimize the situation? Of course it was. And today, we are discussing a trader's tactical instrument like Trailing Stop.

What is Trailing Stop and what is it Used for?

As you know, the Stop Loss is intended to limit the loss in case the price of an instrument has started to move in the losing direction. When the position becomes profitable, you can manually move the SL to the no-loss level or to the level where the SL becomes Stop Profit. In other words, the limit order moves only by following the price movement in the Take Profit direction.

As long as the trader cannot (or does not want) to stay at the terminal all the time, a Trailing Stop is used to automate the trailing process. A Trailing Stop is an optimized version of the Stop Loss, which acts as a dynamic, sliding or floating SL, significantly increasing your profits. Thanks to this instrument, traders can correct their SLs according to the situation and price change, thus protecting their potential profit from unexpected price fluctuations.

This instrument is especially useful in the event of a strong and rapid price movement in one direction, as well as in cases where the trader does not have the opportunity to watch the market all the time.

Working with a Trailing Stop

A Trailing Stop is always linked to the open position, i.e. before initiating a Trailing Stop, the trader must open a position. The Trailing Stop algorithm is performed on the client's terminal, not on the broker's server, as in the case of Stop Loss.

To place a Trailing Stop in MetaTrader 4, open Terminal, then open the context menu and choose Trailing Stop. Then choose the desired distance between the SL and the current price from the dropdown list. Only one Trailing Stop can be placed for each open position.

As soon as these actions are completed, the terminal checks the profitability of the open position for new quotes. When the gain in points equals or exceeds the specified level, a SL is placed automatically.

The order is placed at a predetermined distance from the current market price. Then, if the price movement increases the profitability of the position, the Trailing Stop automatically moves the SL after the price. The order is not modified if the profitability is decreasing. Therefore, the risk level is automatically optimized or the profit is locked. Each automatic SL modification is logged in the system job log.

Trailing Stop can be disabled by selecting **No** in the menu. **Remove All Levels** disables all trailing stops on all open positions and pending orders.

It should always be remembered that a Trailing Stop works on the client terminal but not on the server (like SL or TP). Therefore, if the terminal is powered off, Trailing Stop does not work. If the terminal is off, only the SL will work, placed next to the Trailing Stop.

The Trailing Stop is executed only once with a tick (with a price change). If there is more than one open order with a Trailing Stop for a symbol, only the Trailing Stop of the last opened order is executed.

Note: When placing a Trailing Stop, pay attention to the fact that a pip on accounts with five-digit quotes is not the same as a standard pip. In other words, 40 pips for accounts with four-digit quotes and 40 pips on a terminal with five-digit quotes differ 10 times (4 pips in the four-digit system = 40 pips in the five-digit system).

Example: After the price has moved 40 pips in the chosen direction, reaching 1.12109, the Trailing Stop will automatically move the SL to the no-loss level, which is 1.11709, and if the price continues to rise, it will keep moving the Stop Loss so that it is at 40 price pips.

Trailing Stop as a Trading System Component

Many of you know what it is to follow a position, but most of you have only heard of it. In fact, most new traders are unaware of the difference between following and watching an open position. Well, Trailing Stop is an instrument of the following trades. As a rule, a trailing stop is used in trend or momentum strategies, although it can be used in either.

For example, after the price bounces off the support line of the ascending channel, the trader opens a long position, placing Take Profit near the resistance line and Stop Loss below the last local low. However, as long as the market is not a linear environment and can change the direction of movements randomly, some factors can prevent the price from reaching the TP. The next time the trader looks at the position, they might see a locked loss on the SL (if it has been placed) instead of a profit. However, if the SL has not been placed, this can lead to a serious drop in the event of high volatility.

In real trading, Trailing Stop is not just an algorithm to move the SL automatically. It is a tactical trader maneuver that can be launched manually. However, in such a case, the trader uses a slightly different principle and logic of moves. For this type of trading, Stop and Reverse (SAR) indicators are used, for example, the Parabolic SAR indicator, Volty Channel Stop, Fractals, etc.

Setting a Trailing Stop with the Parabolic SAR Indicator

Set a Trailing Stop with the VoltyChannel_Stop flag

Set a Trailing Stop with Fractals indicator

The use of such indicators could be part of a trading system where the trader does not just choose the level and place a TP. At the same time, if the price goes against the trader's position, the milestone for the SL can move closer to the price to optimize and decrease the possible loss.

The Trailing Stop is a much more flexible and comfortable way to use the Stop Loss. With this instrument, the trader has the opportunity to use the full potential of the market movement, while simultaneously reducing the risk of large losses. Moving the SL automatically following the quotes in the profitable direction for the trader is a serious help in a situation where the trader cannot control the situation by himself.

How to Place a Trailing Stop

A trailing stop is a function that automatically moves the Stop Loss after the price moves a certain distance away from it. This function is accessed in the MT4 Terminal by right clicking. Then, for the Trailing Stop, set the number of pips. As the profit on the open position grows, the SL will move automatically. Please note that for Trailing Stop to work properly, the terminal must be powered on.

In contrast to Stop Loss, Take Profit is not used as much. In these cases, the position is moved to the break-even point. Transferring to breakeven means placing the SL in the positive area, and if triggered, the position is closed at a profit, although we do not use a TP.

Place a trailing stop

How to Automatically Set Stop Loss & Take Profit

At present, there are many programs to make life easier for the trader. Whereas before, Stop Loss and Take Profit had to be manually placed, and the trader had to modernize the order in several steps if they were to be changed. Today, things have become much simpler. Simply left-click on the order on the chart and drag it to the desired price level. A SL or TP will be placed depending on the direction in which the order was moved.

There are scripts and Expert Advisors that automatically place Stop Loss and Take Profit levels based on set criteria for each new order. On the network, you can find an advisor called Auto-MM with a short user guide, which calculates the trading volume and automatically places the Take Profit and Stop Loss.

Many traders neglect the Stop Loss. By trying to close the losing position manually, they begin to feel sorry for the trade and hope that the market will reverse in their desired direction. As a rule, such actions lead to large losses and drawdowns. Meanwhile, a correctly placed Stop Loss helps to limit losses to an affordable level according to the MA.

In certain cases, the use of Take Profit prevents the trader from making more profit. The reason for this is that it is placed a short distance from the level where the position was opened and prevents the price from realizing its full potential for movement.

In order to use protection orders correctly, the trader must study his strategy well and make a decision about the risks in trading before starting to trade.

Conclusion

So far so good, we have discussed the simplest ways to trade trend lines. They are one of the oldest technical analysis tools, but chart traders use them all the time, including them in their trading systems. A breakout of such a line can indicate the end of a strong trend or simply a confirmation of the formation of an inverse chart pattern. Lines are also drawn directly on indicator charts, such as the RSI. As we see, there are many options for trading trend lines, so we should not stick only to the classic approach, trying to create unique trading methods with simple instruments of technical analysis.

We hope that you enjoyed the book and found the contents informative. Do bear in mind that if you want to become a better trader, the only way is to get the education and then put in the time.

That being said, I would like you to do something really quick for us just before you close the book. If you don't mind, please kindly help us out by writing a 5-star positive review on Amazon just for this book. Assisting us with a positive review will encourage us to keep on writing high-quality books like this one that will transform your trading career and the rest of our interested readers. Your 5-star positive review will highly be appreciated.

Thanks for reading and stay blessed!

Printed in Great Britain
by Amazon

23283040R00076